TEACHING PRIMARY SCIENCE

Science from water play

John Bird

A Chelsea College Project sponsored by the Nuffield
Foundation and the Social Science Research Council

Published for Chelsea College, University of London,
by Macdonald Educational, London and Milwaukee

First published in Great Britain in 1976 by
Macdonald & Co (Publishers) Ltd
Maxwell House
74 Worship Street
London EC2A 2EN

Reprinted 1977, 1978, 1979, 1981, 1983

ISBN 0 356 05071 8

Library of Congress Catalog Card Number
77-82984

Project team

Project organizer : John Bird

Team members :   Dorothy Diamond (full-time)
                   Keith Geary
                   Don Plimmer
                   Ed Catherall

Evaluators :   Ted Johnston
                   Tom Robertson

Editors

Penny Butler
Macdonald Educational

John Pettit
Nuffield Foundation Science Teaching Project
Publications Department

Printed in Great Britain by
Butler & Tanner Ltd, Frome and London

General preface

The books published under the series title Teaching Primary Science are the work of the College Curriculum Science Studies project. This project is sponsored jointly by the Nuffield Foundation and the Social Science Research Council. It aims to provide support and guidance to students who are about to teach science in primary schools.

Although the College Curriculum Science Studies materials have been produced with the student teacher very much in mind, we suggest that they will also be of use to teachers and to lecturers or advisers—in fact to anyone with an interest in primary school science. Hence this series of books.

Three main questions are considered important:

What is science?

Why teach science?

How does one teach science?

A very broad view is taken of teacher training. Training does not, and should not, stop once an in-service or college course has been completed, but can and does take place on a self-help basis in the classroom. In each context, however, we consider that it works best through the combined effects of:

1 Science Science activities studied practically at the teacher's level before use in class.

2 Children Observation of children's scientific activities and their responses to particular methods of teaching and class organization.

3 Teachers Consideration of the methods used by colleagues in the classroom.

4 Resources A study of materials useful in the teaching of science.

5 Discussion and thought A critical consideration of the *what*, the *why* and the *how* of science teaching, on the basis of these experiences. This is particularly important because we feel that there is no one way of teaching any more than there is any one totally satisfactory solution to a scientific problem. It is a question of the individual teacher having to make the 'best' choice available to him in a particular situation.

To help with this choice there are, at frequent intervals, special points to consider; these are marked by a coloured tint. We hope that they will stimulate answers to such questions as 'How did this teacher approach a teaching problem? Did it work for him? Would it work for me? What have I done in a situation like that?' In this way the reader can look critically at his own experience and share it by discussion with colleagues.

All our books reflect this five-fold pattern of experiences, although there are differences of emphasis. For example, some lay more stress on particular science topics and others on teaching methods.

In addition, there is a lecturers' guide *Students, teachers and science* which deals specifically with different methods and approaches suitable for the college or in-service course in primary science but, like the other books in the series, it should be of use to students and teachers as well as to lecturers.

Contents

Introduction

Play has been described (by Dearden) as a 'non-serious and self-contained activity which we engage in just for the satisfaction involved in it'. But what starts as play can lead on to science. Water, which offers enormous potential for play, also provides many opportunities for scientific investigations.

The teacher's main problem is to recognize what science is coming, or might come, from some aspect of water play. This book is to help the teacher with this recognition. It deals in detail with two topics: floating and sinking, and capacity and volume, expanding on two suggestions in Science 5/13 *Early experiences*. Many further ideas are suggested in Chapter 8.

Because water play is so often a feature of the infant classroom the emphasis throughout is on children aged between five and seven or eight, although many of the ideas suggested are appropriate for older children and even for adults.

As an understanding of science comes best from personal involvement, we recommend that the teacher or student should try the activities and consider them from the children's point of view before using them in class.

Activities with water can all too easily swing towards one or other extreme. It may become all play with very little teacher involvement, as one teacher put it 'A "Who can get wettest?" competition'. Or it may become a rather narrow, rigidly directed exercise from which the children derive little satisfaction. To balance these extremes the teacher must consider what he (or more often, she) would like the children to achieve and how he can help them by means of the apparatus and materials he provides and by the organization of the classroom.

See bibliography: 13, 25.

1 Apparatus and organization

The water container

Children *are* influenced by the apparatus they have. What apparatus you give them depends on what you want them to do, what is available and what you can afford. Certainly, though, you will need a water container.

Containers

Sinks Children usually have access from only one side. This may be a limitation or an advantage.

Water trays Children can get to these from all sides. There may be a commercially produced water tray in the classroom. If there isn't one, and you can't buy one, use washing-up bowls. Rectangular bowls are best as they fit economically onto a bench or table.

Often the type of container you use depends simply on what is available. But where you do have a choice this can have a significant effect on how the children react. Here are some points raised in a discussion between a lecturer and two infants teachers.

Lecturer: 'Which would you choose if you had the chance, a fixed sink or a water tray?'
Andrea: 'Well, given a choice I'd have both. You want free access to running water at a sink, but the advantage of a free water tray is that they can get all the way around it and you're not confined. But I think the fact that we have sinks in the classroom, they're so used to them that this reduces the mess problem.'
Julia: 'The advantage of a water tray is that it's just for water play. The trouble with the sink is—it happened to

me this morning—that a child washed her paint brushes in the sink and the children were then playing with purple-tinted water.'
Andrea: 'Yes, we specially dyed some water blue so that we could do some experiments about air, and the blue water as the day went on changed from purple to black to a very dirty brown, but they could still see the air bubbling up. It is a disadvantage: it is better obviously to have both.'
Julia: 'Conversation you've got to take into account as well. Perhaps children talk more when they are able to talk around. You know, two or three small children leaning over talking round a thing.'

Water trays There are numerous water trays on the market, but they vary greatly in price and suitability. In many schools the water tray is used very rarely, or else just for storing odds and ends. One reason may be that it is designed badly. So if you ever have the chance of buying a tray, the following guidelines may help.

Shape and transparency   With a *long* tray children can sail boats a satisfying distance and enjoy having races, but are much more likely to split into two groups.

A *circular* tray allows more children to stand around it, and they are much more likely to stay in one group.

Small, deep trays may restrict children's play too much.

Transparent containers are far better than opaque ones. It is much more exciting and instructive if the children can look through the sides at what is going on.

The frame   This needs to be sturdy and corrosion-resistant (for example, with a stove enamel finish). Also in crowded classrooms it is useful if the frame can be folded and put away.

Mobility   It is a great help if the whole unit can be moved about, although it is better for the teacher's peace of mind if the children cannot do so easily. Many water trays have castors, but only on two of the legs.

Look at the description of various water trays in a catalogue (see bibliography: 31, 32, 33). Which type do you think is best? What are the main problems and advantages of the water container you use?

Selection of apparatus and materials

A good argument in favour of selecting the apparatus and materials you give to children is that play in the classroom is most useful if it is structured. The children have a free choice of the materials available. The selection is made by the teacher. The children need enough to occupy them, but too much makes it difficult for them to choose what to use.

For instance, a child might be allowed to play with water for a specific reason: to clarify his ideas on capacity. Therefore he needs plenty of containers of different sizes and shapes, and a funnel.

But there is also a strong argument against selection of a narrow range of materials because it provides too few opportunities for the children's interests to emerge. Perhaps there is a case for alternating between the use of materials covering a wide range of possibilities and sets of materials selected to serve a special purpose, as above.

Taking floating and sinking as one example, consider what special sets of apparatus and materials you might introduce and what objectives each might serve. (See Chapter 3.)

What are your views about the need for careful selection of apparatus and materials? Have you any examples you can use to illustrate your case?

Costing

How much does the equipment (excluding the water tray) cost?

Consider the items suggested on pages 24–25 for work on capacity and volume. Use equipment catalogues to find what the total cost might be.

See bibliography: 31, 32, 33.

How far can the cost be reduced by using kitchen odds and ends and by buying locally?

Positioning

Where should the water play area be? if it is not to be round the sink, it should go where:

It can be kept in view.
Access is easy from all sides.
It interferes least with children moving round the classroom.
Mess is least troublesome.

What problems would you anticipate if the water play area is placed in the following way?

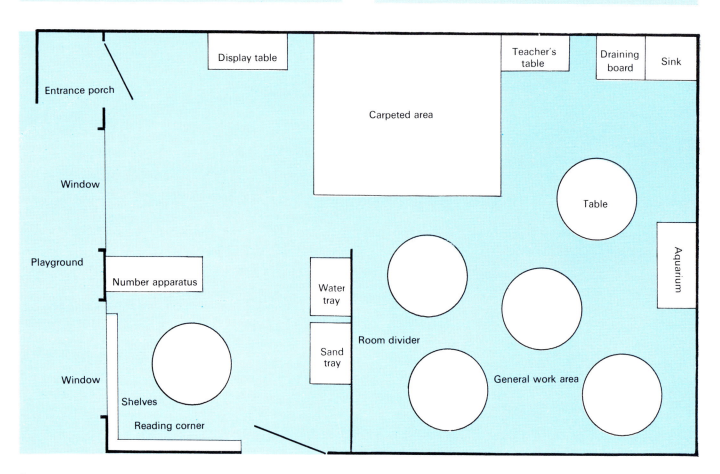

Beginning

Before you start off you will need to decide:

The size of the group or groups.

Which children will do water play.

How, if at all, you will change the groups around.

What other class activities will be going on at the same time.

Methods of communication: for example, might workcards be useful with older children?

Your decisions may depend upon:

How much equipment you have.

Keeping the interest of the children.

Extending the older or more able children.

The interest supplied by other activities. Do these compete effectively with the interest of water play?

With these points in mind, assess the following examples.

Teacher A, with a class of six-year-olds, had started a group of four children on water play. The rest were doing number work, reading and painting. The children round the water tray were playing happily, but were continually being distracted by some of the other children in the class who wanted to join in. What could or should this teacher do?

Teacher B, in a family grouped class with a rich variety of activities going on, had talked to one group of children about some things they might try to find out during water play. They had started enthusiastically, but as they went on the older children kept coming up to tell her what they had done and to ask her what they might do next. Was this something she should encourage

or perhaps just accept? Or could she do something about it?

Teacher C, with a class of older infants, organized her water play at the end of the morning for whichever children had finished their assignments in number, reading or writing. Was this a sound idea?

Class discussion and water play

Water play can be linked with class discussions. In these the teacher talks to the whole class or a large group at the same time, perhaps carrying out practical activities in front of the children to provide firsthand material for discussion.

The class discussion is valuable because it enables the whole class to benefit from discoveries which might otherwise go unnoticed, except by a small group. To some extent also it serves different objectives from water play. Of course, playing with water is the only way of giving children direct sensory experience, but the more structured setting of a class discussion can help the children to develop experimental skills, their ideas and their explanations.

Why use class discussion? Here are some aims of class discussion suggested by a teacher:

To share the discovery of one child with the others.
To get children's ideas and explanations.
To give children information and ideas.
To give children guidelines for future work.
To show them how to test their ideas by experiment.

And, as she put it, 'Let's not kid ourselves, it's purely and simply to save time!'

What are your views on class discussion? Can it be used too much? What special purposes do you think it serves? To help answer these questions it might help to tape-record a session and to follow the detailed flow of the discussion.

2 Classification: what floats and what sinks?

What happens when . . .?

Scientific activity may be roughly divided into two closely related phases. The first, which can be called the 'What happens when . . . ?' phase, is a period of active and seemingly haphazard exploration. It is most evident in situations which are novel and unfamiliar to children or adults. Children seem to need this general experience before they are able to isolate a particular problem and suggest explanations and experiments (phase 2).

Children often start with the questions 'What floats?', 'What sinks?'. You will need as many different familiar objects as you can muster, for instance:

Objects made of metal, wood or plastic
Objects of different shapes and sizes
Containers, such as detergent bottles and yoghurt cartons
Objects with small air spaces, like sponges

Building up general ideas

One special feature of this first phase is the opportunity it gives children to build up general ideas (generalizations) by picking out similarities between different observations. This is especially because of the range and variety of the experiences it provides.

For instance, Elizabeth (aged six) had been playing for

some time with a number of things which included:

A glass bottle which sank even when empty
Glass marbles

Wooden building bricks ⎫
A plastic spoon ⎪
A plastic box ⎬ which all floated
A wooden boat ⎪
Plastic bricks ⎭

Elizabeth's general idea was that 'Plastic things float and wood things float.' This had emerged without conscious help from the teacher, who had made suggestions and asked questions without this end in mind.

Floaters or sinkers?

Building up generalizations involves classification. For example, take the problem of which things float and which things sink. This seems very simple, but it may be beyond young children. Also is it really all that easy for adults to predict what will happen to some objects?

Here is a challenge: you will need a miscellaneous collection of plastic objects, rubbers, steel wool.

Try them out. How successful were your predictions? Work out some trick problems like a table-tennis ball wrapped in Plasticine. What about using this in the classroom? It could give rise to interesting discussion.

Of course children will have seen at the bottom of water things like boats which have sunk or have been sunk: This will lead to the problem of how floating objects can be made to sink, and how objects on the bottom can be made to float again. Children enjoy testing this during play.

Trying this out With the materials you have available test how many ways you can make different things sink or float. It is surprising how many ways there are. You could list the objects and the methods you used. Bear your results in mind for using in the classroom later.

A poster made by some infants showing the position of various objects in water (see page 10)

A case history

The 'What happens when . . . ?' phase is well illustrated by Philip and Clive, two six-year-olds at a Kent primary school, when they were playing for about twenty minutes. The play was not completely spontaneous as the boys acted on several suggestions made by the teacher. Clearly, however, they were at a stage when they would not have taken kindly to a long and detailed consideration of one problem. For this reason the teacher did not try to hold things up for too long, otherwise interest and, perhaps, control would have waned.

Philip and Clive tried to find ways of making different things float and sink.

1   They pushed a table-tennis ball under water and watched it rise to the surface.

2   They sank a plastic lid by loading it with marbles. They also tried to sink it by capsizing it, turning it over, and blowing at it. They did not succeed.

3   They tried to sink a sponge by squeezing it under water. They were not successful but they did make it sink lower. They noted the sponge changed colour when it became waterlogged.

4   They loaded a sandwich box with many objects and eventually sank it.

5   Clive, who had brought a working model of a diver to school, spent the time blowing air into it to make it float, or sucking water *in* to make it sink.

6   Meanwhile, Philip was squeezing a detergent bottle under the surface and filling it with water so that it would sink. It didn't.

Analysis   This play could be analysed under the following headings.

Things   The objects or situations they explored, for example the ball, the lid, the sponge, the sandwich box.

Activities   What they did or tried to find out. Here Philip and Clive seemed to be asking 'What happens when . . . ?' as they applied various tests without necessarily having any initial ideas about what might happen. This is characteristic, but is not the only activity during this phase. (See also page 29.)

Ideas   The ideas likely to be extended or clarified by these activities, in this case floating and sinking and the factors controlling them.

Turn to page 29 for a list of things, activities and ideas specially relevant to water play.

Imagining
7   Philip 'acquired' the diver and pretended that it was searching the bottom for buried treasure.

This involved at least one activity, imagining, one of the main driving forces for play. But there were at least two ideas involved. Look for these in the list on page 29. As a clue, consider what exactly was happening when Clive was filling the diver and the detergent bottle with water.

Making first boots

Philip and Clive then tried to make various kinds of boat.

8   They tried to make a Plasticine boat that floated. They found this difficult because although they got the idea of giving the boat sides, they always made them too thick.

9   They put a short bamboo mast on the boat. It pierced the bottom of the boat, which in any case would have sunk. As it did so, air bubbles came out of the top of the mast of the wreck.

10   They made a boat out of a piece of expanded polystyrene. Philip added a mast made of a cork and a nail, and the boat capsized. He then fixed a piece of wood using a nail under the boat, which floated upright. When he added a Plasticine sail to the mast the boat again capsized.

11   Philip made a mast out of a large nail and then fixed a smaller nail underneath. The boat capsized and did a somersault in the water.

This sequence involved the same activities and ideas as before, but there were others too. 'Making' figured prominently, but there was also the general idea of 'stability'. Can you see where this is involved? (See also page 21.)

Can children classify consistently?

Many infants are quite unable to see that objects have consistent properties, either in different situations or from one moment to the next.

Some typical comments are:

(about a piece of wood, before testing): 'It stays on top.'
(about another piece): 'It will go under.'
(about a piece of wire): 'Look, it goes to the bottom.'
(about the same piece, later): 'It will float.'

Children may also define the words 'float' and 'sink' differently from adults. For instance they may consider that an object which is just submerged has sunk.

Some infants produced a poster (see page 7) showing the position of various objects in the water. The teacher describes what happened:

'Martin would not have his ball placed on top of the water level. He insisted that although the ball floated it was half under the water. This was a good observation. A class discussion was called and he explained why he had put the ball in its position on the poster.'

Consult *A Child's Eye View* by Mary Sime for a discussion of the early problems young children have with classification (see bibliography: 29).

Discuss with the children their ideas about what floats and what sinks. Did you in fact find that some children could not classify objects into one or other group consistently?

Where they could, how well were they able to predict what would happen? Also, were any problems raised about what precisely the words 'float' and 'sink' mean?

3 Explanation: why do objects float or sink?

When Elizabeth said 'Plastic things float and wood things float' (page 6) she was pursuing a line of questioning started and developed by the teacher. On hearing this comment the teacher suggested that Elizabeth should put a plastic container, with the top removed, in the water. Elizabeth at first predicted that it would float (because it was plastic). In fact it sank.

Teacher: 'Oh, it's gone under, Elizabeth. Now why?' (Pause)
Elizabeth: 'Don't know.'
Teacher: 'Just try it again . . . what's happening now?'
Elizabeth: 'Bubbles.'
Teacher: 'What's going in?'
Elizabeth: 'Water.'
Teacher: 'Do you think the water's got anything to do with it?'
Elizabeth: 'The water goes in so it makes it heavier.'

This was Elizabeth's explanation.

Anyone who has followed a school science course might be excused for thinking that any one observation has only one possible explanation. In fact, of course, an observation can be explained in many ways. Which way is most useful depends on an individual's knowledge and experience and on the extent to which it adds real meaning to his observations.

There follow some of the explanations which children may give. The sequence roughly corresponds to the children's development. But sometimes more than one explanation will be combined in the same discussion in the classroom.

Single factors

At first children may say that things float or sink because of any one of a number of factors. Some adjectives that children may suggest are: 'flat', 'long', 'thin', 'small', 'big', 'light', or 'heavy'.

Contradictory instances   Instances can always be found that will contradict each suggestion. For example, if children claim that something sinks because it is 'heavy', it is easy to find examples of 'heavy' things that float.

You will need some objects which vary a great deal in shape, weight, size, etc.

Look at them and think about what single factors children might claim cause them to float or sink. Then look for observations or tests which would throw doubt on each suggestion.

Your own investigations no doubt show how many contradictions are raised by this type of explanation.

Which factors *do* seem to help determine whether or not an object floats or sinks? Which factors seem irrelevant?

Can children tell weight from size?   During the phase when children explain things by single factors, they are beginning to see that weight and size have a special significance. But they may be unable to distinguish between them: they may identify big with heavy and small with light. This produces many contradictions.

Materials

Children sometimes claim that things float or sink because of what they are made of (see page 6). A few things such as candles, butter and ice cubes float in water because they are made of a 'light' material. Some things sink because they are made of a 'heavy' material such as stone, metal or glass. For example:

Teacher: 'Will the pencil sink?'
Child: 'Yes.'
Child (when it doesn't): 'Perhaps all the wood things float.'
Teacher: 'What about this marble?'
Child: 'It'll sink—'cause it's glass.'

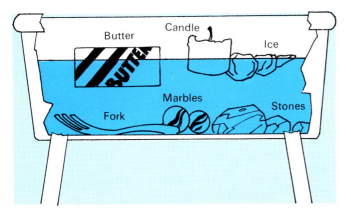

Testing materials   You will need objects made of stone and metal, expanded polystyrene, different kinds of wood, plastic, glass, cork, rubber.

Test all the objects made of one type of material. Are there any cases where this explanation seems to break down? For example, do certain materials like plastic always float? Are there exceptions? Might this be because some plastics are heavier than others? What other factors may make objects made of a heavy material float, or those of a light material sink?

Study this extract from Nuffield Junior Science *Teacher's Guide 1* (see bibliography: 8, page 17).

'Paul, aged five years and three months, was busy putting a collection of objects into water to see if they would float. He announced that a glass bottle had sunk, and when he was asked if he thought all glass bottles would sink he said, "Yes". When a very large bottle was seen to float, Paul said it was because it was shiny. When a shiny steel triangle sank, he said this was "because it's metal". When a tin lid floated it was "because it's round".'

What types of explanation was Paul using here?

Light and heavy materials   Children may simply observe that a particular material, such as wood, always seems to float. But when they make this observation they *may* say that certain materials are 'light' and others 'heavy'. This suggests a growing ability on their part to appreciate that some things are light and others heavy *in relation to their size* (relative weight or density).

In these early stages this idea can only be very hazy. If it is to be fully understood there must be a clear grasp of the ideas of conservation of weight and volume.

See bibliography: 27.

Consider this teacher's conversation with Elizabeth (six):

Elizabeth: 'Water's going in [to the pen top].'
Teacher: 'But the pen top is still floating.'

Elizabeth: 'Well, it's very light.'
Teacher: 'Lighter than the pencil case [which had filled with water and sunk]?'
Elizabeth: 'Yes.'
Teacher: 'What will happen to this ball?'
Elizabeth: 'It'll float.'
Teacher: 'Why?'
Elizabeth: ''Cause it's plastic.'
Teacher: 'What about this plastic spoon?'
Elizabeth: 'It'll float.'
(She puts it on the water carefully and the handle sinks under the surface, the spoon part remaining on top.)
Teacher: 'Why's that?'
Elizabeth: 'This part of the spoon (pointing to the handle) is very light so it sinks. This part doesn't.'

What types of explanation is Elizabeth using here? Has she any notion at all of relative weight? As a clue, note her remarks about the pen top. What does she mean when she refers to the spoon handle as sinking because it is very light?

Air: an important material

Of all the materials air has a special significance in explanations of floating and sinking. This is because so many things that float contain it, even though they may be made of a heavy material like glass or rubber.

Hollow objects with air in the space   Some objects have a large space with air inside. You will need:

Toy balls, tennis and table-tennis balls
Empty bottles
Airtight empty tins
Detergent bottles
Balloons
Soft-drink cans

How best can children test the idea that these objects float because of air in the central space?

One method is to take two containers of the same volume. Fill one with liquid, and leave the other empty. Take, for example, two soft-drink cans, one full and the other empty, and put them in the same water container. Pick out both cans and feel their weights. Now the empty can has an opening and if water is allowed to enter, the can will eventually sink. But of course at the same time this means letting air out.

Apply this test to other objects. Try closed bottles (full and empty), balls, detergent bottles and balloons.

Can you find any things that are full of water and yet still float? If you do, how would you explain this? Has it anything to do with the material of which the container is made?

It is easy to assume that children appreciate that hollow objects contain air. But younger children may find this idea difficult to grasp.

A class discussion Here is an infants teacher's description of a class discussion.

'I asked if a bottle full of water would float. They answered "No". I asked if an identical empty bottle would float; they said "Yes". "Why?" was my next question. "Because one is empty and one is full," was the answer.

'So I asked "If we took all the furniture out of the classroom and then we all left, would the room be empty?" They said "Yes". "What is up above us and all around?" I asked. Eventually we got round to air. I held the empty bottle under water and we watched and listened to the bubbles coming out. One little girl remembered that she'd done a similar thing at home with an upturned glass, she'd "made bubbles".

'We then said that the bottle had air in it. I half filled the bottle with water and it floated under water. We talked about the water pushing air out and displacing it. Then someone mentioned submarines and we were away, discussing how a submarine dives and surfaces.'

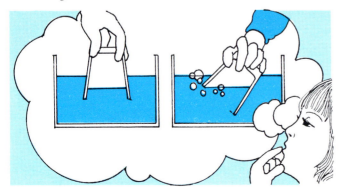

Spongy materials You will need a variety of materials which contain small holes or spaces. Some examples that come to mind are coke fuel, sponges, wood, expanded polystyrene, fabrics, steel wool.

Looking for evidence of sponginess First look for holes in the structure of the material.

Hold the object under water. Do air bubbles rise from it? Does it become waterlogged?

Squeeze it. Does the material feel solid, or can it be squeezed and made smaller?

Squeeze it under water. Can you get air out of the material?

The role of air What objects show clearly that air in them makes them float? Such objects will sink when the air is replaced by water. Do you find that this characteristic is shown consistently by *all* spongy objects? For example, are there some objects which, even when all the air has been replaced by water, will still float?

Of course, relatively, air is 'light' and water is 'heavy'. Why might a sponge sink when saturated with water and float when filled with air? What explains the many exceptions to this rule, for example, that a waterlogged sponge still floats? Is it anything to do with the material of which the sponge is made?

Air out—water in

Will it float the same in the sea? (See page 16, for buoyancy.)

How does water affect buoyancy?

You will need:

A spring balance
Large sheets or blocks of expanded polystyrene
Table-tennis balls or tennis balls
Children's toy balls
A number of containers of different capacities,
eg $\frac{1}{2}$ litre, 1 litre
A selection of objects, some of which float and some of
which sink

Upthrust: seeing and feeling
Water exerts an upthrust on objects placed in or on it, and this can often be *felt*. Take a light object such as an expanded polystyrene block and try to push it down into the water. The force needed to do so gives an indication of how great the upthrust can be. Philip and Clive did this with a table-tennis ball (page 8).

The effect of this upthrust can also be *seen*. Take the balls and release them below the surface. Sometimes one can get them to shoot right out of the water. Can you do this? Make a note of things which show this upthrust most strikingly for children.

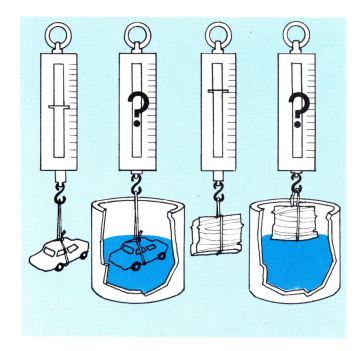

Weighing things in water
Is this upthrust exerted on objects that sink? Take something that normally sinks and hang it on a spring balance, noting the reading on the scale. Then gently lower it into the water while it is still hanging from the balance. Make sure that it does not touch the bottom. Take the reading again. How would you explain the results?

Do the same with an object that floats. Does the result surprise you? If so, consider why an object floats. Is it not because its weight is exactly balanced by the upthrust of the water on it? (See bibliography: 15.)

Perhaps this picture will help your explanation?

Do children think that the 'amount' of water affects buoyancy?
Children and adults frequently think that buoyancy varies according to the volume of water in which an object is floating. This is a surprising suggestion for it implies that a boat will float higher in a lake than in a pond. Work out ways in which children can test this suggestion.

Here is one example: an investigation by Jane, aged seven. Notice how she started this investigation herself.

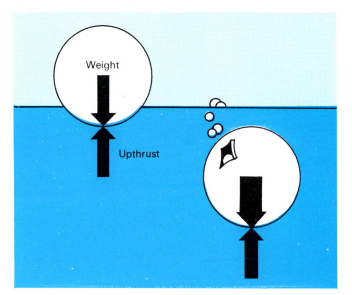

Weight

Upthrust

Teacher: 'What are you doing, Jane?'
Jane: 'I'm trying to see if this pot [a beaker] will float in all of them [a number of beakers of different capacities].'
Teacher: 'Does it float in all of them?'
Jane: 'Yes . . . yes.'
Teacher: 'Are you surprised by that, Jane?'
Jane: 'I expected it to go down in the big one.'

Jane continued to busy herself, and carried out essentially the same type of test on several pieces of expanded polystyrene (which all floated), and on some pieces of Plasticine (which all sank).

What explanation did Jane probably have in mind?

More advanced explanations

Few children are able to go beyond seeing that certain materials float or sink and that water exerts an upthrust on things placed in it. But you may wish to go further and consider more advanced explanations. These are given in detail in most science textbooks, for example *Basic School Physics* by Dean and Edwards, and an excellent book called *The Restlessness of Matter* by L. Basford. One explanation makes use of the idea that an object will float if its density is less, and sink if it is greater, than that of water. To put it in another way, it will float if it is lighter, and sink if it is heavier, than the same volume of water.

See bibliography: 20, 24.

Explain the following:

A detergent bottle still floats even when full of water.

A steel ship floats, but can be sunk.

An object that normally sinks seems to weigh less while hanging on a spring balance and immersed in water, and the weight of a floating object does not register on a spring balance at all.

At the secondary stage, when this type of explanation is often taught formally, children may experience great difficulty. Indeed most adults who have not had a course in physics may find that they have the same problems. (Did you?) Largely this is because this explanation depends upon a clear grasp of volume as well as of weight, and of the relationship between the two (see also page 12). Moreover, comparison of the weight of an object with the weight of an equal volume of water can often only be considered in the abstract.

Consult *Holes, gaps and cavities* for evidence that grammar-school children often find this explanation very difficult.

See bibliography: 14.

Objectives

Here are some Science 5/13 Objectives for children learning science. Are any of these appropriate to water play with children aged between five and seven?

Ability to group things consistently according to chosen or given criteria [for example, those things float/those things sink].
Ability to make comparisons in terms of one property or variable [for example, that is lighter/heavier than . . .].
Awareness that more than one variable may be involved in a particular change [for example, weight and size].
Awareness of properties which materials can have.
Knowledge of differences in properties between and within common groups of materials [for example, glass is heavy, wood floats].
Development of concepts of conservation of [*weight*], *area and volume.*

Have you collected any examples of children's comments which throw light on their understanding of floating and sinking? (A tape-recording would help here.) What general types of explanation do they seem to be using?

Books

Children's explanations of floating and sinking have been well researched. For a detailed, fascinating, but rather complex description read Piaget's and Inhelder's *The Growth of Logical Thinking: from Childhood to* *Adolescence* or *A Teacher's Guide to Reading Piaget* by Brearley and Hitchfield. An interesting chapter in Mary Sime's recent book *A Child's Eye View: Piaget for Young Parents and Teachers*, illustrated copiously with examples of children's conversations, also deals with this topic.

See bibliography: 21, 28, 29.

4 Fair tests: experimenting with boats

In an experiment we try to control the conditions to see if our explanations fit the facts. As at least the older children aged between five and eight are beginning—if only in a rough and ready way—to work out simple experiments, it is important to know what guidance to give. The most important consideration is that an experiment should be fair.

Plasticine boats

This consideration—fairness—can be illustrated with boats made out of a 'heavy' material that normally sinks, such as Plasticine. You will need:

Plenty of Plasticine
A sheet of aluminium foil
Some suitable weights (for example, washers, marbles)
Scissors
A washing-up bowl or water tray

Adults testing
The hypothesis   First, the teacher should put herself in the children's shoes and test the explanation that Plasticine boats float because they possess a particular shape. How might she set about doing this? First work out a hypothesis (sometimes called an 'If . . . then . . .' statement) which expresses the explanation in such a way that it can be put to the test: '*If* the shape has anything to do with it, *then* Plasticine moulded into certain shapes will float, and moulded into other shapes will sink, *all other things being equal*.' It may help to refer to the description of Philip and Clive's efforts with Plasticine boats in Chapter 2, page 9.

The test   Now test this hypothesis, trying to test as many shapes as possible, just as children do, not just the obvious ones. Before doing so, however, note the phrase 'all other things being equal'. Unless other things *are* made equal the results may be open to different interpretations. If all the shapes have different weights it is difficult to disentangle the effect of weight from that of shape. If the test is to be fair, the factor (variable) of weight needs to be held equal (controlled).

What were your results?

Children testing   Most young children find it difficult to devise fair tests. In one class the teacher worked out with the children this fair test: she 'made a boat that floated, then one that didn't, *using the same lump of Plasticine*. We discussed why. Someone suggested a difference in weight so out came the balance.'

It is likely that these children were unable to conserve weight, thinking that it changed with the change in shape even though the lump of Plasticine was the same. *It is difficult for children to take into account factors which they do not fully understand*. This is not to say, however, that this test had no value. How might it have helped?

What loads can boats carry?

Adults testing: Plasticine boats What kind of Plasticine boat holds the greatest load? First the teacher must think of what factors (variables) might be involved (for example, shape, weight), then various hypotheses, and then ways of putting these to the test as fairly as possible.

What were the results and conclusions?

Children testing: polystyrene trays *The manipulation of the factors in a fair test* is also very difficult for children, but with careful guidance from the teacher they can become more competent.

Here is a teacher's report about some infants trying to find out what load two different sizes of polystyrene tray can carry:

'After one session we compared the children's results. They didn't all have the same answers. Could they all be correct? A class discussion seemed necessary. We discussed the need to load carefully, to avoid tossing

the marbles in and capsizing the vessel, and to allow it to fill up with water and sink. We noticed that the larger tray needed more marbles to sink it.'

Class discussion was an important method of guidance here (see page 5).

What factors was the teacher trying to control to make the test fair? What alternative to marbles would you suggest? If there were no alternative, what would you have done?

More tests Now try out tests similar to those here and page 19, using boats of aluminium foil. This material can be folded quite easily without needing to be cut first.

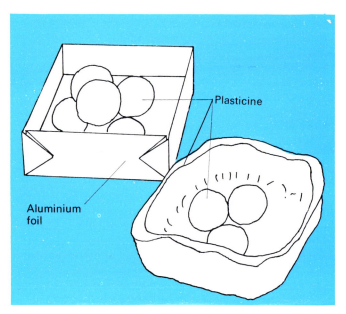

Plasticine

Aluminium foil

Compare the load needed to sink a boat of aluminium foil and a Plasticine boat of similar size and shape.

What difficulties did you experience in either case in working out a fair test? Remembering these difficulties, how cautious should your conclusions be?

Boats made from unsinkable materials

You will need:

An expanded polystyrene ceiling tile
Sheets of 6 mm balsa
Cocktail sticks (be careful with the pointed ends)
Washers for cargo
Coloured paper for sails
Small nails or tacks
A hot wire polystyrene cutter (plus battery)
Scissors
A junior hacksaw

First cut out small square rafts of expanded polystyrene and balsa. What load is needed to sink each type? What will you need to make the tests comparable? Can the tests be made completely fair? It is difficult to keep the load on and prevent it slipping off. How can you overcome this problem? Look at the *Junior Science Source Book* (see bibliography: 5) for two possible solutions.

Stability

Making boats often raises the problem of stability. How do they become unstable? More stable?

Cut out a rectangle of expanded polystyrene or balsa to a scale that fits in with the size of a cocktail-stick mast. Fix the mast in position. What can you do to make the boat unstable? Make the boat shorter or narrower? Change the position of the mast? There are a number of hypotheses. Test each of these and others in turn, trying to keep the tests fair. Then consider how the boat, once made unstable, can be made to regain its stability.

Another factor likely to limit young children's experiments is their *manipulative ability*. Which of the activities suggested above do you think would present manipulative problems to children at the lower and upper ends of the five-to-eight age range?

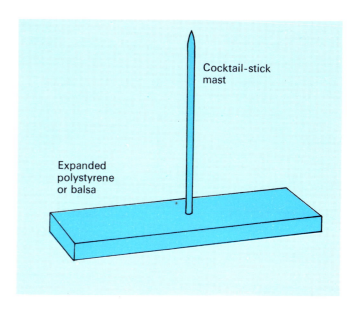

Expanded polystyrene or balsa

Cocktail-stick mast

For safety, tape the point of the cocktail stick.

A difficult test

How much the teacher does for children of a given age will depend upon how far she considers the children can understand what they are doing, the difficulties of working out suitable tests, and the manipulative problems involved. She may choose class discussion (see page 5). Or, careful not to force children beyond their capabilities, she may wait for an opportune moment to suggest an experiment. Here she can supply materials which both raise a problem and provide the means by which the children can solve it. Here is an example.

You will need:

Some sheets of 6 mm balsa
Rubber bands
Some thin dowel rod
Paper or card for sails
A selection of bolts for ballast
A hand drill, with a bit (of same diameter as—or slightly smaller than—dowel rod)
A junior hacksaw

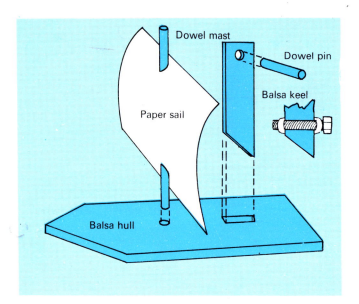

Dowel mast
Dowel pin
Balsa keel
Paper sail
Balsa hull

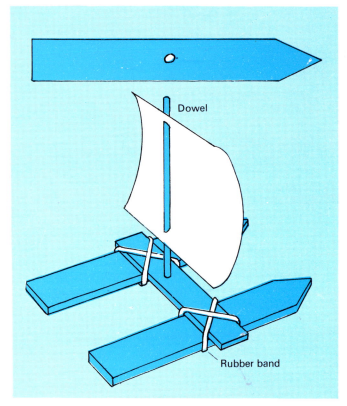

Dowel
Rubber band

Make a yacht to this general design, making sure that it is just narrow enough to float upright in the water but will capsize easily when blown along. Make a keel and a slot through which it can pass through the deck of the boat.

Make two boats of the same size and shape which will not stay upright when masts are fitted. Also make a cross-piece with a hole for a mast. A stable catamaran can be made by fixing the cross-piece to the two keels with rubber bands (see opposite).

A teacher describes what she did with these models:

'The children were left with the equipment for a few minutes but without instruction. They tried to use the yacht, but without much success. I joined them and was told that the boats didn't work. We compared the yacht with a picture of a yacht and they noticed that the keel in the picture yacht was missing on our model. I showed them how to fit the keel to the boat. They played a while longer and I asked them if the boats were still capsizing. They said "Not always but sometimes." We studied the picture of the yacht again and found that the ballast on the picture was missing on the model. We fixed the bolt on the keel and made our self-righting yacht. They found the two narrow boats useless so I showed them how to form a catamaran.'

The effect of shape   Turn to *Early experiences*, pages 22–23 (see bibliography: 13). Consider the idea of testing how the shape of the boats affects the way they move. Which boats show the effect of streamlining most strikingly? Does the difference show up best if the boat is made of a wood that is dense and sinks low in the water? How fair do you think your tests were?

For further ideas refer to *Science from toys*, pages 38–51; *Early experiences*, pages 22–23; and *Holes, gaps and cavities*, pages 23–24. (See bibliography: 13, 14, 17.)

What difficulties did you find in helping children of this age group to work out 'simple' tests? Did you in fact encounter difficulties in understanding, in working out fair tests, and in manipulative ability? If so, what form did these problems take?

5 Capacity and volume

One of the interesting things about working on capacity and volume is that children often think that the amount of water increases or decreases as the water moves from one container to another. It is important, then, to find out what they mean by the word 'amount'.

Here are some questions as starting points.

How many times will one container have to be filled in order to fill another container? For example, how many milk bottles full of water might be needed to fill a bucket? And how many to fill a detergent bottle? In this way the approximate nature of measuring becomes more apparent.

Look at some bottles and jars. Can you pick out which holds most, least, the same?

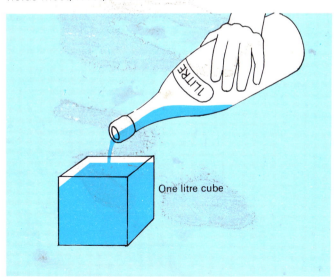

One litre cube

Some explanations of the word 'amount'

One idea that is frequently used by children when they are pouring water from one container to another is that of conservation. Broadly, children have some grasp of this idea if they can understand that the quantity of liquid does not change even though its shape does. But the form and level of children's grasp of the idea of conservation may vary greatly and may lead to explanations which attach different meanings to the word 'amount'.

Here are three explanations which suggest some differences in meaning.

'It's the same lot of water as you started with so it must be the same amount.' Here, amount means quantity of substance. Children argue that no 'stuff' could have

disappeared during transfer (conservation of substance).

'It's a different amount because it's higher/lower (according to the shape of the container).' In this case the child is comparing only *one* factor or variable, that is, the height of water in the container.

'It's the same amount because although it's higher/lower it's also thinner/fatter.' Here the child is taking into account the relationship between two variables, height and cross-sectional area.

Infants are perhaps most likely to give the second type of explanation, possibly combining it with the first. The third explanation may come later, but is still far from the implication that water occupies *the same amount of space* in different containers (conservation of volume).

For further illustrations of the growth of children's ideas about conservation of substance and volume refer to *The Growth of Basic Mathematical and Scientific Concepts in Children* by K. Lovell. Note how essentially the same principles apply to solids like sand, as well as to liquids. (See bibliography: 27.)

Here is a case history from Nuffield Junior Science *Teacher's Guide 1* (see bibliography: 8).

'Christopher (aged five) was filling a plastic milk bottle from a jug. When the bottle was brimful of water the jug was still half full, but when asked Christopher said the bottle held more. Further questioning showed that by "holds more" Christopher meant "is fuller". It transpired that he knew which vessel had the greater volume, but had failed to understand the question because of his limited vocabulary. Again, this does not mean he should not have had this experience—that was how he had learned to express a notion about volume correctly, and he could not have learnt in any other way.'

This example shows the importance of careful questioning to clarify what children mean. Which of the three types of explanation described above was Christopher closest to, judging by his use of the phrase 'is fuller'? Do *you* think Christopher 'knew' which vessel had the greatest volume?

Apparatus

To extend the range of possibilities you could build up a collection of empty plastic containers of various shapes and sizes. These might include containers which:

Vary in diameter from top to bottom, for example some shampoo bottles.

Do not vary in diameter from top to bottom, for example detergent bottles.

Vary in cross-section, for example oblong, triangular and round ones.

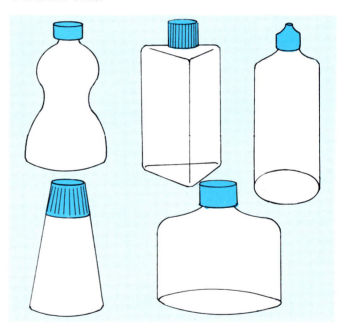

Refer to educational supply catalogues and look for the following:

Cans and bottles   You might collect containers holding standard quantities of a litre or a pint, for example beer cans, wine bottles and milk bottles. Especially useful is a set of bottles of the same capacity but different shape. These can sometimes be purchased from educational suppliers.

Note: because of the dangers of breakage glass bottles should only be used when they are particularly appropriate. You can make the jagged edges on cans harmless with adhesive plaster.

Funnels   At least one large and one small one. They are quite cheap but you can make them by cutting the tops off detergent bottles or gallon or half-gallon containers of lemonade or detergent.

Buckets   It is helpful if these can be graduated.

Measuring jugs   Transparent jugs with graduations are probably best.

Measuring beakers   are in sets of different capacities up to a litre with graduations on the outside.

Liquid measures   are made of aluminium and are not usually graduated. Like the measuring beakers they are made in capacities up to one litre.

Capacity cubes   are made of plastic and in capacities up to one litre. Because they are fragile they cannot be used for water play, but they are very valuable during class discussions.

See bibliography: 31, 32, 33.

Filling and emptying things

Filling things accurately   Children spend much of their time filling and emptying containers in water play. One thing they can learn from this activity is how to fill things accurately. Graham (aged five) had learnt this. He had been given a new set of plastic milk bottles, ten in all, and spent a long time filling each to the very top. Proud of his competence he lined them up near the sink and never returned to them again.

How can you encourage children to achieve such competence?

What do 'full' and 'empty' mean?   There is then the question of how to define fullness and emptiness. Obviously they are only loose concepts: is a bottle ever completely full or empty? Perhaps one should aim at developing the notion that things are very full, nearly full, fuller than, and so on. Consider some practical ways in which you can help to build up this idea in discussion with children.

Why do things need to be full or empty?   We often fill or empty containers because we are using them for measurement. This enables us to make sure that we are giving or receiving similar quantities of material. Unless our standards of what fullness means are reasonably consistent this will lead to unfairness and inaccuracy.

Consider:

Two children playing at 'lemonade', filling several plastic cups from a jug.

One child using a plastic cup as a measure of the difference in capacity of two detergent bottles.

What situations might arise that would enable you to stress the value of the idea of fullness (and emptiness) in measuring?

Unusual problems

Collect apparatus for children to investigate the capacities of containers:

Holding less (than shorter ones in a set) The more striking the difference in height and capacity the better.

Of the same height, but different capacities These might include containers with the same cross-section from top to bottom as well as containers whose cross-section varies.

Of different heights, but the same capacity You could try:

Bottles, such as wine bottles.
Plastic containers of widely differing shapes cut down so that they have the same capacity.
A combination of different types, for example, litre bottles and a cube of one litre capacity (see page 23).

When asked about the categories above, children might well say about each of them:

'The tall one holds more.'
'They all hold the same.'
'They all hold different amounts.'

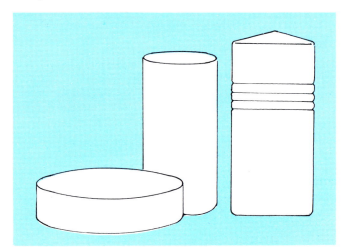

What might they mean by 'more', 'the same' and 'different'? What questions could you ask to find out? What activities or observations could you suggest that would help to throw doubt on these explanations?

Consult *Beginnings* for a discussion of many of the problems of teaching capacity (see bibliography: 9).

The scale of measurement

You will find it helpful to mark as many containers as possible showing divisions of a quarter, a half, and three-quarters of the capacity. If the cross-section is constant from top to bottom, marks placed at equal distances measure equal quantities. This might be illustrated by preparing three containers, thus:

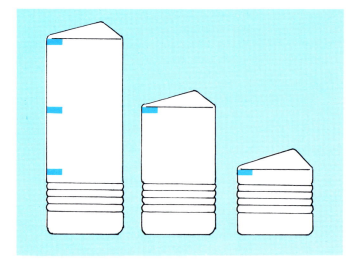

If you place marks at equal distances on a container varying in cross-section from top to bottom, how could children be helped to see that in this case marks equal distances apart do not measure the same amount?

What other methods might you use to illustrate this point with children?

Objectives

Here is an extract from a taped discussion with some children at an infants school in Devon:

Teacher: 'I'm going to make sure that it [water] *all* goes in.'
Anne (aged five): 'That's less.'
Anthea (aged six): 'Because that's fatter.'
Teacher: 'Now, let's put it all back in here. I'm not going to waste any.'

She poured it to and fro between a fat squash bottle and a thin squash bottle, during which a disjointed conversation occurred. Then she suggested pouring it into a half-gallon plastic can.

Martin (aged five and a half): 'That one's got more room in it 'cause it's fatter.'
Anthea: 'It'll only be a little in that one because it's so fat. It's ever so fat.'
Teacher: 'Rachel. Have I got the same amount of water in here as I had in there?'
Rachel (aged four and three-quarters): 'No.'
Teacher: 'If I hadn't got it in here where did it go?'
Rachel: 'I don't know.'
Ivan (just five): 'It went 'cause it's fatter.'
Teacher: 'Have I got the same amount of water in here as I had in there, Ivan?'
Ivan: 'No. It's gone 'cause it's fatter.'

Examine the children's comments carefully. For this activity at least, which of the following objectives seem to have been satisfied, and with which children?

Development of concepts of conservation [of length] and substance.
Ability to make comparisons in terms of one property or variable [for example, the height of water in different containers].
Awareness that more than one variable may be involved in a particular change [for example, that diameter is important as well as height].

Development of concepts of conservation of [weight, area and] volume.

Are there any children whose replies suggest that they are confused? Does the conversation illustrate anything about the value of discussion?

Understanding conservation

It is sometimes suggested that a child's understanding develops in a rough sequence which is controlled less by experience and learning than by the rate of his or her maturation.

The implication of this theory is that you cannot introduce children to concepts such as conservation *before they are ready.*

In *The Philosophy of Primary Education* Dearden questions this idea of readiness. How much do you think the idea of maturation can and should be applied to the idea of conservation? (See bibliography: 25.)

Have you examples of your pupils' comments which may help to throw light on their understanding of conservation?

Goods displayed in shops provide a possible direct application of the idea of conservation to everyday life. Such displays encourage us to be mesmerized by the most immediately obvious variables (for example, tallness) and therefore to make a bad choice.

Of course, if we understand the conservation of volume we will not necessarily choose correctly, but we are more likely to. Moreover, a scientific training which has consistently encouraged children to look beyond the immediately obvious, and to acknowledge the existence of other important variables, will help them to react cautiously when making many day-to-day decisions.

6 Points of interest

Science should be fun. It is almost inevitable that initially children will derive enjoyment and satisfaction from water play. But how can these be maintained? One way is to link water play with children's everyday experiences. Essentially this means transforming a situation into a form which means something to the children.

The teacher can use these points of interest both as starting points, at the beginning of an activity, and at appropriate moments as the work goes on.

Stories   Here are some examples from work on floating and sinking and capacity, together with comments the teacher might make.

Noah's Ark   'What do you think must have happened when the elephant stepped on the Ark?'

Aesop's fable, 'The Crow and the Pitcher'   'The crow *was* clever. He dropped stones in to make the water come up to the mouth of the pitcher where he could drink it. Say he had put corks in instead of stones, would this have done the trick?'

'Why the Hippopotamus Took to the Water'
(from Rhoda Power's *Seven Minute Tales*)   'What other animals live in the water? How can they float?'

See bibliography: 10.

Pictures   A set of clear pictures from magazines or colour supplements makes good talking points for odd moments.

Here are some suggestions.

Submarines: 'How can they go up and down in the water?'
Sinking ships: 'What makes boats sink?'
Ducks and swans: 'How can they float so well on the water?'
The aquarium: 'Which animals can you see that can float?' 'How much water do you need to half fill the aquarium?'

Experiences out of school
Food: 'If you had different sized mugs, how could your mum make sure all your family had the same amount of lemonade?' 'Can you think of any things you eat that float?'

Swimming: 'Is it easy to float?' 'What can you use to keep you up?'

Supermarkets: 'Does the tallest bottle always contain the most stuff?'

Fishing: 'How do you keep the float down in the water?'

Competitions: 'Who can make a Plasticine boat that holds ten marbles?' 'Who can find the container that holds the most?'

For practice, work out some points of interest based on boats or any other topic that appeals to you.

What points of interest did you use for discussing water play? From your discussions with the children, what everyday interests emerged that you had not thought of before?

7 Putting ideas together

Practical activities with young children are bound to give rise to interesting problems which are often quite unforeseen. So compelling is young children's interest that, almost inevitably, the teacher will try to develop some of these points, although the ones selected will depend upon her own interests, experience and objectives.

A checklist

It is also a help if the teacher has a picture of the direction in which the discussion and investigation might go, given a particular starting point.

For this purpose it may be useful to have a checklist of possibilities.

These may consist of:

Things   Objects or phenomena that children might usefully discuss or investigate.

Activities   What children can do or try to find out.

Ideas   Ideas which are specially likely to be extended and clarified through study of this topic.

Here are some examples from this book. No doubt you can think of many others.

Indeed, a teacher who becomes familiar with the items in it can use them to stimulate discussion and investigations in any situation irrespective of the topic, for example the use of comparison—saying to children 'What's it like ?', 'What's it different from ?'.

Things
Water
Materials (eg wood, metal)
Air
Boats
Submarines
Divers
Containers (eg bottles)
Laundry

Stories
Pictures
Food and drink
Shops and supermarkets
Animals (eg fish, whales)
Aquaria
Bubbles
Siphons

Activities
Observing
Generalizing
Comparing
Classifying
Explaining

Measuring
Making
Painting and drawing
Imagining
Writing about

Ideas
Weight
Size
Dimension : length, width, etc
Shape
Floating
Sinking
Upthrust
Density
Streamlining

Stability
Capacity
Displacement
Horizontality
Pressure
Capillary action
Absorption
Surface area
Evaporation

Flow charts

Each of the three lists on this page can be read quite simply as it stands. Also, many useful ideas can come by putting together items in or from each list, and by making flow charts.

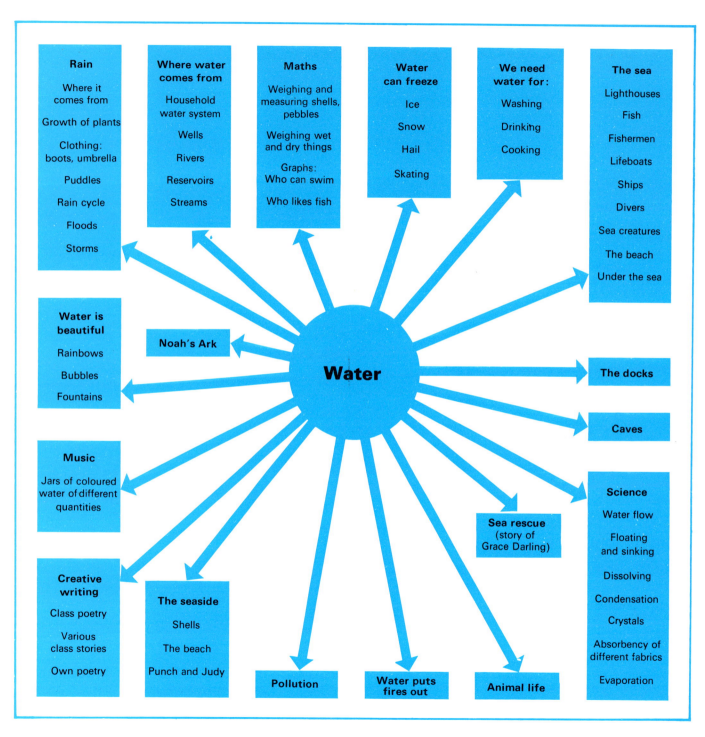

Rain

Where it comes from

Growth of plants

Clothing: boots, umbrella

Puddles

Rain cycle

Floods

Storms

Where water comes from

Household water system

Wells

Rivers

Reservoirs

Streams

Maths

Weighing and measuring shells, pebbles

Weighing wet and dry things

Graphs: Who can swim

Who likes fish

Water can freeze

Ice

Snow

Hail

Skating

We need water for:

Washing

Drinking

Cooking

The sea

Lighthouses

Fish

Fishermen

Lifeboats

Ships

Divers

Sea creatures

The beach

Under the sea

Water is beautiful

Rainbows

Bubbles

Fountains

Noah's Ark

Water

The docks

Caves

Music

Jars of coloured water of different quantities

Science

Water flow

Floating and sinking

Dissolving

Condensation

Crystals

Absorbency of different fabrics

Evaporation

Sea rescue (story of Grace Darling)

Creative writing

Class poetry

Various class stories

Own poetry

The seaside

Shells

The beach

Punch and Judy

Pollution

Water puts fires out

Animal life

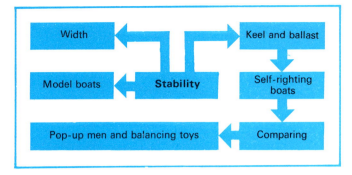

Of course, in searching for ideas no holds are barred and any method that gets results is valid. Nevertheless, this method may help the search, particularly if it is linked to the use of the bibliography.

In the example above play with model boats (*things*) leads to the *ideas* of stability and width. These in turn lead to the *activity* of comparison with the pop-up men and balancing toys.

Here is an example of a flow chart based on the topic 'Our Aquarium'.

The chart on page 30 was used in a primary school.

Practise making a flow chart for yourself based on things that float and sink or capacity. Then try a less familiar topic like bubbles. Use it as a basis for discussion with the children. What discussion and investigations followed? What other ideas did the children suggest?

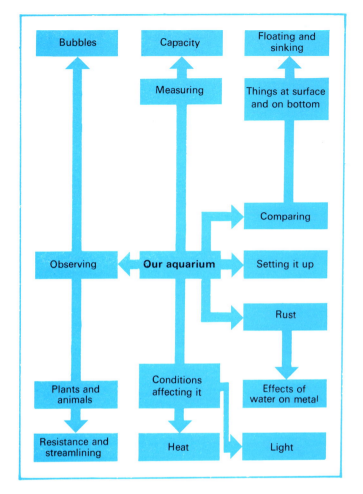

8 More things to do

Here are some further ideas for activities. Try these and look for ways of initiating or extending these ideas with children during water play.

Making bubbles

You will need:

Plastic tubing
Drinking straws
Sponges
Cloth
Plastic bottles
Balloons
Yoghurt cartons

How many ways can you find of making bubbles in water? Children often think that bubbles are empty space. What is the best way to suggest that they contain air? Children might also think that the bubbles disappear when they reach the surface. What might you do to show that something is released when the bubble pops? (See bibliography: 30.)

Air and water

You will need:

Bottles
Plastic coffee cups
Jam jars
Plastic tubing
Detergent bottles
Semi-transparent funnels

1   Float a cork, or another buoyant object, on the water. Take a jar and lower it mouth downwards into the water over the cork. Continue to lower the jar. What happens? Does the cork remain level with the mouth of the jar?

Explain what you observe.

2   With your thumb tightly over the hole in the stem of a large funnel lower the funnel, mouth downwards, into the water. You should observe the same effect as in nos 1 and 4. Now release your thumb. What happens, and why?

Two useful ideas here are:

That air, even though invisible, takes up space.

That water exerts pressure on the air in the funnel. This pressure increases with depth.

3   Lower a jar, A, into water and fill it with water by tilting it upwards. Then raise it with the mouth downwards until only the mouth remains below the water surface. Surprised? Now tilt the bottle until part of the mouth comes out of the water. What happens?

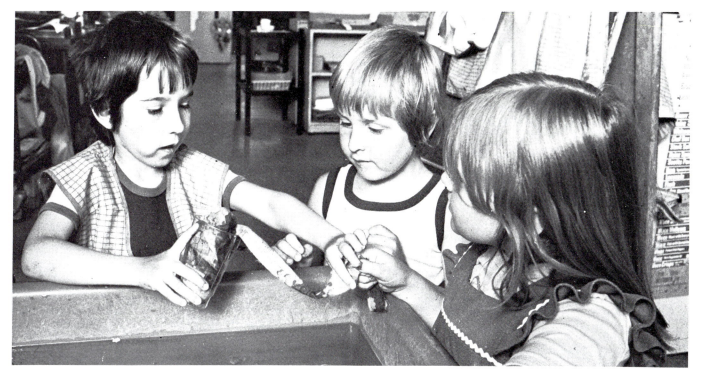

4   Wedge a piece of paper or cloth tightly into the bottom of a jar. Then lower it mouth downwards into the water. What do you observe? How do you explain this? (The diving bell works on the same principle.) (See bibliography: 14.)

5   Fill jar A once again and hold it, mouth downwards, and full of water. Lower another jar, B, mouth downwards into the water and tilt it so that the bubbles it releases rise into jar A. Obviously air goes from B to A, but what else happens at the same time?

6   Make a hole with a nail near the bottom of a detergent bottle. Fill the bottle with water. Hold your thumb over the mouth of the bottle; keeping it there, raise the bottle out of the water. Then take your thumb off.

7   Take two jars with tightly fitting lids. One jar has two holes, the other has one hole, pierced in the lid. Which of the two jars is easier to fill or empty?

8   Suck water into a plastic tube. Quickly place your finger over the free end. Then raise the tube completely out of the water. Take your finger off the end. What happens and why?

A simple explanation of these activities is that water and air each tend to *displace* the other. Water cannot leave unless air can enter. Air cannot leave unless water can take its place.

There are many other everyday examples that help to illustrate this idea. Thus, you need to bore two holes in a can before the liquid can flow out easily. There is also a 'right' and a 'wrong' way to drink liquid from a lemonade bottle (see bibliography: 13, 20).

How can you make the above point with children? Obviously the more experiences they can have of this type, the better. Questioning which takes the form 'What is coming out?' and 'What is going in?' might also be better than a direct explanation. How easily do you think the children understand what is happening?

Water finding its own level

You will need:

Plastic tubing
Rubber tubing
Two funnels
Various containers

1   Pour water into transparent containers of various shapes until they are about half full. What happens when they are tilted? The answer seems obvious. Nevertheless, just to check up, look carefully to see what happens to the water as the containers are tilted.

2   Insert a plastic funnel at each end of a length of rubber or plastic tubing. Fill the system until there is water in both funnels. Then raise and lower each funnel in turn. What happens? What general rule can you work out for the level of water in both funnels?

Do young children find this phenomenon easy to understand? You might ask them to predict what happens before you tilt a container or raise the funnel. What variety of answers do you get?

Children's ideas of the horizontal and the vertical have been studied by Piaget.

See bibliography: 21.

Water flowing out

You will need:

A detergent bottle
Plastic tubing
Two transparent or semi-transparent containers (for example, measuring jugs)

1   Bore a line of small holes at regular intervals from top to bottom in a detergent bottle. Fill with water and allow the water to flow through the holes. What do you observe?

2 Children should know how to make a simple siphon. It has a number of real uses such as emptying the class aquarium, but take care that the children's enthusiasm does not get the better of them.

Half fill the two containers with water, placing one higher than the other. Suck water up into the tube from the upper container until the tube is completely full. Quickly place your finger over the free end of the tube. Place this end below the water level in the lower container and release your finger. Water will then flow from the upper to the lower container. Raise and lower each container. What effect does this have on the direction of the flow? Can you position the containers in such a way that the flow of water ceases? What happens if you introduce a large air bubble into the tube? Does the siphon *still* work?

Water will flow through the tube from a higher to a lower level. A good explanation of siphoning can be found in *Water* by D. M. Chillingworth (see bibliography: 23).

This explanation, while not difficult for adults, will be beyond most children. However, they might observe and appreciate the *rules* governing the flow of water. How far did you find that they were able to grasp these?

Water in and on things

You will need :

Bricks
Pieces of wood
Various fabrics
Various papers, including waxed and blotting paper
A glass dropper

1   Place drops of water on different materials, including fabrics and papers. Try also wood and bricks. Which surfaces absorb water easily, and which with difficulty ?

An artist's adaptation of some children's work on drops

Drops on different surfaces

I made some drops on silver paper and some look like pebbles and some look like eggs and some look like stars

I made some drops on silver paper and some are like stones and some are round and some are big

I made drops on a piece of wood They made a pool

I made some drops on a piece of wood They looked like a dog

I put some drops on some material I could not see them

I made some drops on polystryne They did not soak in The drops did look like

I made these drops on greaseproof paper some look like mountains some look like beads The drops soaked in the paper

I made some drops on formica. The drops look like swimming pools

2   Place strips of cloth or fabric with one end in water and leave for some time. Try other things like string or cotton. What happens ? Some factors involved in absorption may be the presence of holes or the tendency of the material itself to take in water. Water may rise through absorbent materials because it can 'climb up' the tiny holes by capillary action. (See bibliography : 11.) Such features are often hard or impossible to see. It is therefore more a question of discussing possibilities with children and of generalizing to other situations, than drawing hard and fast conclusions. Consider, for example, the absorption of water by sand or soil, or the use of capillary watering in the cultivation of potted plants.

3   Sometimes water is held up on the surface and is not absorbed. You might look to see how the shape of the drops varies on different surfaces. Also, what is the effect on the shape of the drop if you add detergent to it ?

See bibliography : 13, 14.

Drying

You will need:

Some pieces of thin cloth
Strips of paper
Saucer
Tall narrow container
Two identical containers with airtight caps
Tablespoon

1 Cut the cloth or paper into strips of equal area, then soak in water. Try out the effects of various treatments on the rate of drying. For example, you might try:

A radiator
Hanging a strip in a draught
Placing a strip in a closed bottle.

2 Try some experiments with standing water. For example, half fill a jar with water and screw the lid down. Pour an identical quantity of water into another jar and leave the lid off. Leave for a day or so and see what has happened. Also pour a tablespoonful of water into a saucer and into a tall narrow container. What happens after a day or two? (See bibliography: 13, 23.)

Some factors that affect the rate at which water evaporates are:

Heat.
How moist the atmosphere is (usually moister in an enclosed space because the water vapour can't get away).
Whether the air is still or moving.
The surface area.

The effect of all of these factors can be observed by such tests. What other familiar experiences can you think of that would help children appreciate the factors that affect the rate of drying? Above is one experience you might draw on to help children appreciate that water doesn't just disappear when it evaporates. Can you think of others?

Consult the bibliography (11, 23, 30) for further ideas.

In developing these and other ideas in the class, what similar experiences can you introduce that will help children build up general ideas? It helps to say to children, 'What is it like?', 'How is it different?'. Also, as in Chapter 6, consider what everyday experiences you can use to stimulate interest.

What types of explanation do the children give? What form does their testing take? How effective are these tests?

Bibliography

For children to use

1 Pemberton, John Leigh- (1973) *Ducks and Swans*. Ladybird Books. Wills & Hepworth.
2 Scott, Nancy (1966) *Pond Life*. Ladybird Books. Wills & Hepworth.
3 Usborne, P. (1972) *Under the Sea*. Macdonald Zero Books. Macdonald Educational.
4 Webster, James (1973) *Water*. Ladybird Books. Wills & Hepworth.

For direct work with children

5 Bainbridge, J. W., Stockdale, R. W. and Wastnedge, E. R. (1970) *Junior Science Source Book*. Collins. See pages 130–131, 134, 198–200.
6 Dixon, D. (1967) *The School Aquarium*. School Natural Science Society, Publication No. 9.
7 Hollings, M. (1968) *Water for the Under Eights*. School Natural Science Society, Publication No. 31.
8 Nuffield Junior Science (1967) *Teacher's Guide 1*. Collins.
9 Nuffield Mathematics Project (1970) *Beginnings*. Chambers/John Murray. See pages 8–9, 11, 67.
10 Power, Rhoda (1971) *Seven Minute Tales*. Evans Bros.
11 Rosenfeld, Sam (1968) *Science Experiments with Water*. Faber.
12 Schools Council Science 5/13 (1973) *Change*, Stages 1 and 2 and background. Macdonald Educational. See pages 21–22, 43–45, 59.
13 Schools Council Science 5/13 (1972) *Early experiences*. Macdonald Educational. See pages 22–23, 50–51, 65–66, 84–89.
14 Schools Council Science 5/13 (1973) *Holes, gaps and cavities*, Stages 1 and 2. Macdonald Educational. See pages 22, 23–24, 26–28, 34–37.
15 Schools Council Science 5/13 (1973) *Like and unlike*, Stages 1, 2 and 3. Macdonald Educational. See pages 12–13, 52–53.
16 Schools Council Science 5/13 (1973) *Metals*, Stages 1 and 2. Macdonald Educational. See pages 49–50.
17 Schools Council Science 5/13 (1972) *Science from toys*, Stages 1 and 2 and background. Macdonald Educational. See pages 25, 38–40, 43, 44, 67.
18 Schools Council Science 5/13 (1972) *Time*, Stages 1 and 2 and background. Macdonald Educational. See pages 14–15.
19 Schools Council Science 5/13 (1972) *Working with wood*, Stages 1 and 2. Macdonald Educational. See pages 27–31.

For further information and ideas

20 Basford, L. (1966) *The Restlessness of Matter*. Foundations of Science Library : The Physical Sciences VI. Ginn & Co. Boston. See pages 66–70.
21 Brearley, M. and Hitchfield, E. (1970) *A Teacher's Guide to Reading Piaget*. Routledge & Kegan Paul Paperback. See pages 73–106, 107–110.
22 Britton, James (1971) *Language and Learning*. Allen Lane (now Longman). See pages 162–163.
23 Chillingworth, D. M. (1962) *Water*. Chatto Educational.
24 Dean, K. J. and Edwards, N. E. (1969) *Basic School Physics*. Blackie.
25 Dearden, R. F. (1970) *The Philosophy of Primary Education*. Routledge & Kegan Paul. See pages 29–32, 95–105.

26 Holloway, G. E. T. (1967) *An Introduction to the Child's Conception of Geometry*. Routledge & Kegan Paul. See pages 65–68.
27 Lovell, K. (1966) *The Growth of Basic Mathematical and Scientific Concepts in Children*. University of London Press. See pages 61–68, 69–77.
28 Piaget, Jean, and Inhelder, Barbel (1958) *The Growth of Logical Thinking: from Childhood to Adolescence*. Routledge & Kegan Paul. See pages 20–45.
29 Sime, Mary (1973) *A Child's Eye View: Piaget for Young Parents and Teachers*. Thames & Hudson. See pages 58–64.
30 Unesco (1970) *Source Book for Science Teaching*. H.M.S.O.

Catalogues

These can be obtained from various suppliers of school equipment, among them:

31 E. J. Arnold, Butterley St, Leeds LS10 1AX
32 ESA Creative Learning Ltd, Pinnacles, P.O. Box 22, Harlow, Essex CM19 5AY
33 James Galt & Co. Ltd, Brookfield Rd, Cheadle, Cheshire SK8 2PN

Acknowledgements

The author and publishers gratefully acknowledge the
help given by:

P. Davies, Warden of Honiton Teachers' Centre, Honiton, Devon

The staff and children of:

Brookfield County Primary Infants School, Larkfield, Kent
Sherbrooke Primary Infants and Junior School, London SW6
Sidmouth County Infants School, Sidmouth, Devon
Tidemill Infants School, London SE8

Illustration credits
Photographs
John Bird, page 7
Kevin Morgan, pages 2, 15 (bottom)
Terry Williams, all other photographs

Line drawings by GWA Design Consultants

Cover design by GWA Design Consultants